Crystals for the Empath

Beginner Guide to Healing Crystals
By Contessa Miller

Welcome to the world of Healing Crystals.

These beautiful amazing Energy beings have been waiting to connect with you.
This book is meant to open your heart to the Healing Crystals bring.
Many believe crystals are incarnations of the Divine.

Crystals are all around us.They pull you close to work with them.
Crystals are used in our watches, our computers,and microwaves.
We use crystals,often and are totally unaware of it.
The first thing a crystal communicates is that it is an efficient tool for energy,enhancement & spiritual growth. Each is working uniquely according to your vibration;Not to mention they are beautiful!
Why can't we "hear them?" They have a "vibration" to them that you can feel.

After environmental factors, the most common cause of personal energy depletion is family, friends & clients. Needy people "hook" into subtle bodies in your aura (energy around the body, emotionally ,mentally ,karmic or spiritual) Here they gain the nourishment, They are what is called a" Psychic Vampire" (taking energy not blood)You will often feel tired or drained.
When your vibration is high your chakra's are aligned you will know and feel the work of your crystals.You will feel the vortex of positive life.
Crystals are key holders to unlocking & balancing your blocked or depleted energy. Each one calls us in times of need for true inner work,balance & clarity.

Crystals also come in many sizes and forms.When picking a crystal ,go for what "feels" right to you. You will be surprised time after time which one calls to you.

"I must have this rock" you might think when you first catch sight of one.
I know the feeling. Once you add a crystal to your environment, that's it!

Lots of people also do not understand the healing that comes from crystal energy and might have negative thoughts or remarks about crystals without really understanding them.Taking the time to understand crystals can be a wonderful spiritual tool, helping to heal, up lift and change your life.

This book is meant as a quick guide to get to know your stones,chakra's, and aura. This way you can meditate with them and expand on what you already know inside.Your journey with crystals will transform you on many levels. Leaving you no doubt as to your beauty,your gifts. They will challenge you to make tough choices to better your life.
Crystals are wonderful tools to use, they are sacred in healing. They have a way to give you guidance, as well as wisdom,awakening you to love yourself deeply.
As you dive deeper into this love, It also brings love to the earth and everyone around you.
The Energy of the Crystals helps you to open your eyes to any unwanted behavior, toxic thoughts or needed awareness.

Crystals *work with your intentions.The highest good. This is good to keep in mind when feeling for the right crystal*

Bringing your Crystals Home:

This is such a special time,when you connect to a crystal the energy is felt right away,remember-the crystal also picked YOU

1.Use Sea salt or Pink Himalayan salt in a bowl over night.

2. Sage or incense to clear energy left on the crystal.
Light the Sage or incense, blow out flame, wave crystal in smoke.

3.Make your intention known as to how you will work together.
always with love.Bring intention to mind for the crystal.
Some crystal are not meant to be placed under water, for this reason.

4.Use other stones- to charge- Selenite or Black tourmaline.

Crystals can come in to contact with many people before coming to you.The use of sage clears the energy.

During full moon night to let them sit outside in the light this helps them clear out the "Old Energy".Let them soak up moon light to reenergizing them this allows clearing.
Many people and places have come in contact with stone, this clears away energy to work with you.

Aura's

The term "Aura" is used to describe parts of our body that can't be seen with a naked eye rather.For many Empaths the aura can be seen or felt. Today new Photo's can be taken of your Aura.

Many people spend their lives only aware of the physical body, They feel emotions in limited or oversensitive ways.Empath's take on the energy of others like a sponge. Crystals help transform this energy for healing.

It's your "Personal Space"-Where we feel our emotions like, Anger, Hate,Joy, Happiness. This is why we say things like
" She wears her emotions on her sleeve". Understanding where Empaths hold emotions is key to releasing them.

People can become "oversensitive", meaning they feel all emotions around them very intensely, whether it's their own, or they picked up others emotions.Many call this Empathy.

Crystal help with the over sensitive Empathic people, Crystals show to be very helpful and useful in allowing the body more balance in its way of sensing energy and transmuting it.This allows you to open up, becoming aware of the energy on all levels.

Layers of Aura	Location	Connection
The Emotional	Closest to the body 1-5 cm	Damage results in Illness Connection to family, Fitting in
The Mental	5-10 Cm away from body	Rational mind, intellect Self esteem
The Astral	10-20 cm from body	unconditional love, Self hate,environment Self worth
The Etheric	30-40 cm from body	Connection to communication Spiritual ,angels
The Celestial	90-190 cm from body	Environment,past and future
The Divine	all	Love,Energy,Divine Knowledge What we hope to achieve

What Is the Aura?

The Aura is made up of different levels or layers. The body has an energy field that is made up of seven layers, linking the seven chakras. Each has its own vibrational frequency. Each layer is lighter then the next.Some very gifted people will see the layers or gray matter in detail.

1. The Emotional Aura
This is the Energy you feel when you hug someone or "Feel" if they are sad or happy.

2. The Mental Aura
This is where our thoughts are stored or where you feel someone is if they are
" Spacey"

3.The Astral Aura
"Spiritual" Aura this is where our consciousness "goes" when we meditate,dream or receive information from your spirit guide or helpers as well as the Angels/Archangels.

4. The Etheric
Healed by expressing your truth,knowing who you are.

5.The Celestial
Third eye connection. brings in unconditional love and light.

6. The Divine
Crown chakra, Psychic awareness.Being one with all that is.
Becoming more sensitive to the layers of your aura is a process that is naturally gradual, or it can happen very fast..Children's sensitivity is very keen. Teens tend to be very loud with there growing and changing aura.As adults we wait to see how a room "feels" or if some one who is happy really "feels" happy. Some close emotions down for fear of what others will "think" which we can "feel" also.
Tapping into your aura is a diving deeper into your intuitive body.
At times you can receive rips or tears in your aura and become sick, It is very important to care for your aura.

Remember crystals work with the energy vibrations to strengthen the Aura layers, release blocks and add healing to levels of spiritual,mental,astral, physical & emotional. This brings Balance.
Low self- Worth and Low Self Esteem can have value and healing.

The Universe is Alive & Has an innate Perfection.

Being aware that everything is energy whether its the chair you you are sitting in, the wind or your home. It is living atoms swirling around.Each thing has its own speed or rate at which it moves. The energy can be positive,negative or neutral. It's how we transmute the energy that counts.

Crystals Vibrate at a Certain Level~ Some are Fast High Vibrations & Some are Slow Grounding Vibrations.
We can see Crystals Being Grouped together like "Cousins" in a Family.
However if your Energy is Negative, It can Vamp that.
Crystals Ask that you Keep a Calm Loving Intention.

Think of how electricity has to move and not be still. The same can be said of the rays of light all around you. Your body even radiates an energy around it and beyond making the aura body.Crystals are more then just beautiful rocks. They conduct energy in many ways.

An amputee will often times experience pain where the amputation has occurred . It is not from the "pain" ,rather,due to the aura & the subconscious mind that the "limb" is still present in the "auric" Field. Using a crystal linked to the limb helps clear and balance the pain.

Your thought's & feelings bring about the state that your aura will be in. Some can feel the aura,some can see the Aura , but most importantly is whether your thoughts make your aura vibration level high or low.We notice an aura changing many times as we talk to some one, feeling if they "Lift their Spirits" or if they are "Feeling Low".Someone in love is lighter and glows a bit. Things seam to just slide off their backs.

Love, kindness, forgiveness & gratitude bring your aura, as well as those around you to a higher Level.

Are Crystals Good for us?

YES! CRYSTALS WORK WHEN WE WORK WITH THEM. THIS CAN BE IN THE FORM OF A PIECE OF JEWELRY HAVING ONE IN YOUR WORK PLACE, OR A TUMBLED STONE IN YOUR POCKET. MOST OF THE TIME 10-20 MINS IS ALL YOU NEED WITH A STONE TO FEEL THE VIBRATIONS MATCH AND RAISE YOUR VIBRATION.

Tumbled Stones are Great for Beginners.

Crystals with a higher

Remember,
Its a Process
to Healing,
Awareness & manifesting
your
Highest
Good

Faster vibration links us to the higher realms, Angels and Spirit Guides. Lower vibration crystals work on grounding the Energy and bring it back to Mother Earth.

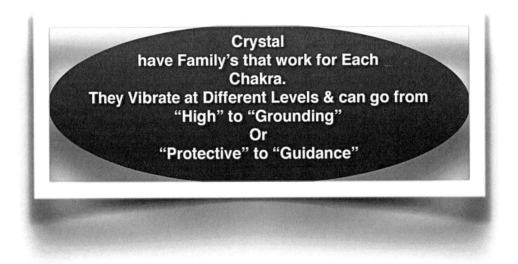

Crystal
have Family's that work for Each
Chakra.
They Vibrate at Different Levels & can go from
"High" to "Grounding"
Or
"Protective" to "Guidance"

Chakra's

Chakra translates to Wheel in Sanskrit.
Your most deep self, The human energy body~
We have inside the body an energy highway of sorts which is called The Chakra system.There are a great many Chakras in your body, Yet 7 remain our main focus. Life force energy inside you spins energy to these centers. They move up your body from Base to Crown.

While getting to know crystals, It is important to learn about the Chakras.This way you will understand the vibrations, and how they will effect your energy as well as the energy all around the world.

It's good to understand the links Chakras have;When they are running smoothly. You are in perfect health , mind, body, spirit. If they are blocked, or over active, dis-ease can come into your life.

Healing our relationship to our inner body takes time and care, It also brings in prevention from illness.If a Chakra is too open, blocked or slowly spinning, your health will experience difficulty.

Base Chakra

It is Located at the base of your spine & controls our Energy of movement and feelings,.It's our foundation of Energy in the body. Linked to our survival,connection to Mother Earth, feeling safe, physical identity & ancestors.

At its core is our survival center- that "Fight or Flight" space we need to have for life from back.We need it every day. It still connects our Energy to our ancestors, how they behaved, and how they over came defeats. All of these memories have been passed down into your subtle bodies and are located in your chakras. It is extremely important to balance your base chakra. This is the space you feel and learn to be safe. This chakra is formed & mostly worked on from birth/womb till seven years of age.

The base chakra is linked to all physical and practical things in Life. This chakra needs to be working in a balanced way for great physical health, financial security.

Like a tree this chakra is your roots to the ground.Anchoring you into the physical world and allowing you to feel safe and grounded. When ungrounded or blocked you will experience emotions being off and physical issues like lower back problems, hip or feet and legs or many have financial blocks.

Sacral Chakra

The Sacral Chakra is located just below the belly button & is our center for pleasure and enjoyment with life. It's about opening up to feelings like connection, sexuality, and emotions.

Transformation occurs on this level to feel changes and experience moments of bliss. In this Chakra we learn that "Losing our Temper" can be frowned on. This is also our space to love our bodies that we are in, to feel connected to them. Passion is found here, creative Energy flows here in all forms.

Linked with water, It shows us to transform or adapt to our surroundings.

When unbalanced your creativity is blocked making feelings of guilt toward intimacy occur, pain, negativity & even shyness. Infertility & reproductive issues can occur here.

This chakra is about Flexibility!

Any type of creative flow or block from art, music, writing or relationship is associated here.

When working strong, confident thoughts, actions and our total vibe is filled with excitement.

it is the energy of childhood, filling it with vitality & opening you to your boundaries.It Develops from 7 to age 14

Solar Plexus Chakra

Sitting just above the belly at the navel, the Solar Plexus chakra is all about our issues we have with personal power! Its the Center where we "Feel" something before it happens. The Solar Chakra helps us when our Emotional body has anxiety, stress or worry.

It is here that we also "Feel" a room & can tell if it is pleasant or if somebody just had a fight. It acts as an antenna or feelers to the rooms or atmosphere that we come in to.

Many psychics / Mediums are very sensitive and open in the solar plexus chakra which means that they can send feel events before they happen.

Ever notice that you cross your arms over your stomach when you're not feeling somebody's energy as being loving? This is a form of protecting your solar chakra. Many people with weight problems whether is bulimia or overeating have an in balance in the chakra.

When we love our bodies have a healthy relationships with food and understand the energy and the environment this chakra is balanced.

From Age 14-21 it is Developing

Heart Chakra

Located in the center of your chest where your heart can be found. This is our self love center, unconditional love space & our strong link between people.
A space where we can bring in love, or feel heart break.
We feel happiness, joy, loved or unloveable, anger, hatred. If closed off, bitterness creeps in.When fully opened, You heal the world with your love.

This Chakra is not always open, as very young we learn to close it off for fear of rejection or vulnerability.
When we open our Heart Chakra, We open up to all the love in the world,we experience love & happiness as well as a level of peace.

When its shut down, we form emotional hurts which lead to "Heartache".
It acts like a filter¯ of love being felt even with out saying a word.
This center is where our "God" or "love" is felt and kept. Where our "Trust" is stored.
Many who have heartache and bad relationships will often times have Heart issues as the Heart Chakra is linked to the flow and energy of love.
Falling in love for the first time is the best way to explain this Chakra. Letting in true compassion to love yourself & Bring in deep inner peace.
Age 21-28

Throat Chakra

Located at our Throats,

This is our energy center linked to communication in all its forms:

Listening, talking, shouting,signing or writing.

This chakra links over the heart at times and regulates energy from the Sacral Chakra to link the creative flow.

When lack of creativity flows,energy in the form of writers block or low motivation can occur.

It can also get blocked if you are putting off talking to someone about your truth or if you are sworn to secrecy.This chakra lets our Expression and communication function.

This chakra if blocked can link to thyroid problems hearing & or shoulder difficulties as well as a hard time expressing personal expression.

When in balance we speak and express what we think and how we feel with ease.It's about your Truth, Connections and creativity.

28-35 years of age

The Third Eye

Located in the middle of your forehead just above your eyes. It is the energy of our visions as well as our thoughts. This is the center of intuition.

In this center "Toxic Thoughts" can change or form how we see things. This is also the center for our "Psychic" gifts & ability.

Not every one will have the same gifts. Opening up to your gift brings light to others. The Third Eye helps us build on our natural gifts. Connecting to wisdom and insight, it helps motivate creativity.

The energy flowing here is our spiritual insight and reflection. This is where you feel your senses, and open up to better choices.

Hitting on inner wisdom, the ability to think is known as " The Sixth Sense" ,a clairaudience or psychic form of "Knowing" .

35-42 years of age.

by Contessa Miller

Crown Chakra

Located at the top of your head. The Crown Chakra our link to Spirit, Spirit Guides , The angel realm as well as the universe.

 A place of pure bliss can be felt here. It's open to allow a gateway to enlightenment and It's best to have all the lower Chakra's working and clear of any negativity or energy blocks.

 To have a great fountain helps when opening your Crown Chakra. If you get off balance here, you can fall in to the "Christ "like state where you feel you are reincarnated as a leader with devastating results .

 If Blocked this Chakra leads to depression, sensitivity to light & Sound, and hopelessness. It also leads profound sadness at not conneccting to source energy/God/love.

 It is at our crown where we receive messages from our guides, and the deeper connection to understanding ourselves.

 The Crown chakra lets us transcend our limits yet connects us to all that is.

42-49 years..

Then the Chakra's at 50 start back to the Base Chakra.

Each crystal has its own vibration and the Chakra that it works with.Some Crystals work on more then one Chakra at a time.

Remember, it's ok to fall in love with a crystal, it's also ok to not enjoy the energy of a crystal and pass it on to someone in need, You might have just been to go between for that crystal.

Amber

Said to be the Tears of God, Amber is tree sap that has cooled millions of years ago. Amber seals any rips or tears in the aura and it Helps maintain any goals you need to reach by brining in Yin & Yang Energy.

 Keep in mind, Amber has a lot of Energy to it & You might that find you "Zap" things when you touch them. Amber is a wonderful stone to use during Break up's to help with Fear and Negative Energy.

Amethyst

A Perfect stone to open "Psychic Gifts".

Or extrasensory perceptions.

Clairvoyance-Clear Seeing,

Clairsentience -Clear feeling

Clairaudient -Clear hearing

Claircognizance- Clear knowing

Clairgustance-Clear tasting

Clears mind of chatter to receive angelic wisdom, protective, linked to Archangel Micheal.Opens crown & Third Eye Chakra's. Helps with all types of additions, overindulgence,& evil thoughts.

Very Calming when anxiety or stress effect challenging situations.

Azurite

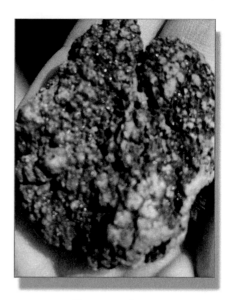

Azurite Opens and Activates your
third eye. This allows you to shine
from within and to share your gifts
with the world in a wonderful
magical way. Azurite is very
powerful at helping you receive messages from the Divine and
it attunes you to interpret messages and signs for your higher
good.

Azurite has links to Throat Chakra clearing tension and
stress.

It is also used to help with achieving a dream state in a
mystical way, to receive wisdom from God/Universe, Angels
and Spirit Guides.

Blue Calcite

Blue Calcite opens your Throat chakra, allowing your voice to be eloquent and link you to psychic communication.
It also clears your ear chakra's to hear divine guidance.Blue Calcite will heal shoulder, neck,and thyroid issues as well as heal those sworn to secrecy. Blue Calcite is also a dreamer stone, lifting your dreams to the astral level allowing for safe travels.
Use Blue Calcite when studying to help retain info.

Blue Lace Agate

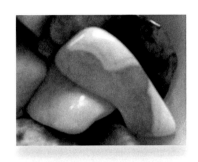

This soft blue and white stone Works deep in your Throat chakra, Letting your words be heard as well as listening when you need to listen. Blue Lace Agate helps by creating a space of calm in your aura allowing you to release stress and maintain balance during your inner journey in an elegant way. It is a stone of communication and confidence. Blue lace Agate helps with how we use our words as swords or words to heal. It also helps by teaching you that delicate can be strong and effective.

Carnelian

Said to be a compass stone,Carnelian is used to always bring your soul back home.It also brings in creativity,gratitude, purpose and abundance.Carnelian is also know to Help with painful

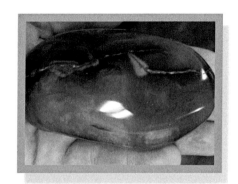

menstruation in women.Works with Gratitude and abundance vibrations.

Carnelian heals the level of your aura just before someone hugs you.

 Carnelian clears that "Personal space" where you hold emotions on your Aura.

 Linked to the Sacral Chakra it has bold energy and Helps with fertility issues.It Heals emotions to be expressed through Throat Chakra and is wonderful for actors as it lifts the voice.Stimulates life force healing lower back issues and anchors you into the now.

Celestite

This stone fills you with peace, angel energy & Illumination.It Helps link you to angels and spirit guides gently for easy communication.

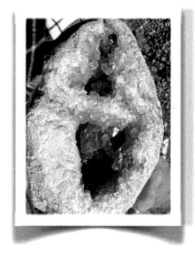

Celestite uses music as it's teacher and is said too vibrate at the sound of Heavens choir.
It lifts our vibration quickly in the form of prayer.
Celestite is linked to throat chakra it serves as a link to angelic communication to speak your truth while opening to levels of consciousness.

Citrine

A stone of true joy and abundance leaving no room for negativity. Clearing and unblocking solar chakra helps to build self esteem & self Worth. This magical yellow stone helps with seasonal depression by adding loving light in the darkest of times.

Citrine cuts out old habits by letting in new abundance in all forms- Friendships, Abundance and Health.Citrine works on deepening your connection to the cosmos and raising your vibration purifying it on many levels.Citrine allows you to receive your universal challenges with ease.It's a perfect stone to keep in your money box!

CLEAR QUARTZ

Clear Quartz clears Negative
energy and expands your
aura.It awakens spiritual
gifts,and purification of your
energy field.Clear Quartz

amplifies energy and transmutes it to assist in any
toxic feelings, run down emotions or to deepen
wisdom. revitalizes the soul, to transform old ways
of thinking to user in the new blessing energy.
Wonderful as a first crystal,Quartz absorbs &
Releases Stress.

Desert Rose

This powerful crystal links you to the universal plan. Letting Feelings of Love and well being rise & grow within you.Desert Rose is said to contain a helpful spirit guardian, growing yourself worth and trust along the  way.It Can be used as a talisman, helping in the teen years to build confidence.Desert Rose is Perfect to increase sensitivity to any psychic gift & abilities.Encourages Friendships and companionship with gentle energy. Desert Rose allows support during grieving periods to deal with emotions.It clears away negativity in thoughts and feelings and brings in more joy.
Desert Rose attunes those wanting to help with sick or older animals.

Dioptase

A stone of compassion & love, Dioptase is used to heal old wounds of abandonment in any life time.

A heart chakra, used in stone healing the emotional pain of break up's & heart ache. It also brings new goals to your life.

Dioptase helps in a bring in vision of higher purpose and to release and let go with new Energy.

Dioptase will also bringing in Prosperity and wealth to many areas of your life.

If you are feeling stuck or find it hard to move in your life this stone brings in forgiveness by letting you see what needs to be let go.

Dioptase helps in breaking down the walls to release negative emotional beliefs that do not serve our higher purpose.

This crystal brings in truth and honesty to relationships on all levels quickly.

Fluorite

Fluorite works on all chakra's and it helps with dizziness and/or Vertigo.

Thought to be a Rainbow in stone form, Fluorite helps to deepen Spiritual goals.

It also helps empower intentions as well as Grounding Energy.

Fluorite is also great for swelling due to fibroid myalgia, Lupus & is very helpful during cancer treatments.

Fluorite clears the astral body of any unwanted entity.

Works on confusion, toxic thoughts and third eye blocks by getting energy flowing.

Hematite

Hematite is a great grounding stone to use any time you need Grounding. Works on the Base chakra.

Helps with Courage & Excitement for life.

Allows you to see the surface of emotions can be different then with-in.

Helps clear Negativity by creating a protective shield around your aura. Builds trust and survival instinct. Wonderful manifestation stone for bringing your dreams to the Earth, Keeping visions true and very helpful for lower back pain.Hematite can be used to help with overcoming additions, trauma's and stress.

Labradorite

Labradorite is perfect to clear mental or toxic thoughts and debris. Assist in discovering Psychic gifts. Enhances Tarot readings, clairvoyants, clairaudience, telepathy,Spirit and higher guide connections.It also opens the Third eye Chakra.Labradorite works as an amplifier for any Healing and is helpful for any past life recall.

A stone of Magic, it adds healing to any inner work that is needed.

Labradorite sits on the corner of timelessness allowing great visions and Helps with Evil eye.

It is a Protective Crystal by removing any hooks or leaks in Aura.

Lapis Lazuli

A very high vibration stone, Lapis Lazuli works on opening your Third eye Chakra as well as opening your inner Temple.It gives a rebirth to intuition as it cleans the third eye chakra.Lapis Lazuli is wonderful if  insomnia is persistent and it will help align you with higher vibrations it clears away toxic thoughts and is great for past life journeys.Lapis Lazuli deepens meditation and vision.It also brings out the inner Queen or King. Lapis Lazuli is said to be the first stone crushed and used as Make up.

Moldavite

This crystal is not of this world and is said to be a meteor. The changes that this stone brings are fast, as you will feel an energy Rush or rather Flush  through your chakra's. Moldavite works at a soul level opening the Heart Chakra. Connecting to ascended masters, spirit guides and Akashic records, letting you become a light bringer. A stone of inner spiritual transformation for your highest good. Moldavite will bring healing where it is needed in your body with ease.

MoonStone

A perfect stone to clear intuition,
bring in self mastery, insight and protection. A feminine stone, it works well with the moon and seeing cycles in your life. Moonstone is great for the traveler by adding positivity to your journey. It helps you see the hidden truths and to recognize when you are letting yourself down. Helps bring in psychic gifts and helps to Lift in times of tiredness or Depression. It also helps to feel a mothering and loving energy.

Onyx

A very grounding crystal, Onyx helps with self mastery, dreams, inner strength and focus.

Onyx is the first crystal to be mentioned in the Holy Bible. It works gradually to help you make new goals and it helps with the discipline to reach those goals.

Onyx helps to relax anxiety in a soothing grounding way and it helps with self control. It also builds confidence when things become a challenge.

Pyrite

Often called Fools gold. This powerful crystal help heal the solar chakra. Bring in

abundance and awareness to the universal flow of Positive energy. Is a masculine stone with it's persistent energy.It works on levels of assertiveness and boundaries of self.Pyrite is great for mastering any type of Fear that "get it done"attitude.Helps with digestion or eating energy blocks.Helps release toxic friendships.

Rose Quartz

This Mother Earth Loving Crystal brings in Heart healing at a deep level.Inner peace and Joy are son to follow  when holding or meditating with this stone. A wonderful helper for fertility treatment and it works wonders on those with hot tempers or anger issues.Rose Quartz helps with depression by allowing self love to come in.

Smoky Quartz

A grounding stone that allows what you need to come closer to you, almost like a magnate.Smoky Quartz is wonderful for any Oracle or Tarot reader,Medium or Empath.It is also wonderful for dream recall and clarity and it works as a transmitter to negative energy.This stone is very protective and Spiritual and allows one to see or feel the energy of auras from those who have crossed over as well as from other Realms.

Selenite

A highly spiritual stone, Selenite clears and activates the Crown Chakra allowing Divine White light in.It clears  Negativity, Fears, and Worries and is great for cutting Energy cords on Aura or in rooms.Selenite links you to Angels, Spirit guides and Higher self. Inspires deep healing.Said to be Archangel Michaels Sword. Do not get Selenite in water as it will dissolve.

Sodalite

A wonderful Stone for
expanding intuition and
opening your Third eye/Brow
Chakra.Sodalite helps with
sleeping and insomnia for
deep dreaming and recall.It
works well for releasing
controlling or addictive
issues.Sodalite

expands your awareness to your
subconscious and brings in your strengths.It
also helps as an oracle talisman for readings.

Tigers Eye

A stone of confidence and protection. Tigers eye works fast at balancing extreme emotions. It helps you remain grounded by clearing out stubborn patterns. Brings in Self worth emotions and allows your unique light to shine. This stone helps when you need to work in groups and is a great abundance stone.

Tourmaline

Great Auric protection stone. Tourmaline helps ward off Jealousy or Evil eye attacks. It clears electromagnetic smog from computers, cel phone and microwaves. Perfect for those  Empaths who suffer from new technology . Great for any lower body or chakra blocks. Tourmaline reduces stress, self judgement and worry by clearing your Etheric body.

Wonderful stone for any hands on healing treatments.

Meditation with Quartz

Get your Quartz Crystal, find a comfortable spot and lets begin. Take three breaths ,slow and deep. If you like you ,can close your eyes for deeper meditation and relaxation. Now take a deeper breath and breathe the air onto your crystal. Feel your return breath as you bring the crystal closer and breath on it again. This links your breath to the crystal and lets you feel the energy back. After three breaths relax more as you connect to the crystal. Hold the intention of love and light all around you. Any feelings or signs coming up let them pass as you relax more deeply with your Crystal. Release any tension, stress, worry, or doubt.Now ask the crystal to begin working with you for your highest good and that of the world.It can be said out loud or just in your mind.

Now imagine yourself in a crystal valley where crystals of all shapes and sizes exist.Feel the growing light from each crystal grow bigger with each breath.Breath in how you are a part of everything.

Allow yourself to feel all the positive and healthy energy.This space is always here for you. It is safe and healing as you connect, beginning to open up to this new exciting moment. Now take a deep breath, feeling connection to your child self, ask your child self if you can give her or him a loving hug.Allow the Crystal energy to connect,expand and clear your aura.

Be safe and feel safe, loved,and connected.

Now thank the crystal,allow time to let the lesson sink in, start to wiggle your fingers and toes, coming back in to the now moment.

Try to do this slowly.Open your eyes.

Take three cleansing breaths in and out.

Sage your crystal one last time.

About the Author.

Contessa Miller is a Reiki Master, Certified Medium, Ordained Minister, You tuber & Crystal intuitive. Empathic since birth Contessa trained as a Healer opening up her Gifts of Clairsentience (Feeling or sensing) Clairvoyance (Clear seeing or Psychic vision), Clairaudience (Clear hearing or Psychic hearing) & Aura Readings (Seeing/ Feeling peoples Auras).
Working with Crystal is her passion.
Married for 20 years & lives in Bakersfield Ca.
A loving Mother to two beautiful Children,
One Serving in The USA Navy overseas.

Many Thanks go to My Husband Jeff Miller for all the Love & my huge Crystal collection!

My Children, Katie & Davyd,who bring so much pride,love and laughter to my life.

Thank you Charlie Heard for your editing help and kindness.

Love to all the Healers in Bakersfield- It's been a wonderful Journey with you!

Thanks to all my Beautiful Crystals-You have made my life so Blessed.

Thanks to all my Youtube,Instagram & Facebook supporters-love you all-to many to name!

All Crystals in book photographed & Owned by Contessa Miller

22293160R00027

Made in the USA
San Bernardino, CA
10 January 2019